Connecticut SUN

by Luke Hanlon

Copyright © 2026 by Press Room Editions. All rights reserved. No part of this book may be used or reproduced in any manner whatsoever, including internet usage, without written permission from the copyright owner, except in the case of brief quotations embodied in critical articles and reviews.

Book design by Kate Liestman
Cover design by Kate Liestman

Photographs ©: Erica Denhoff/Icon Sportswire/AP Images, cover; Maddie Meyer/Getty Images Sport/Getty Images, 4, 7, 8; Peter Cosgrove/AP Images, 10; Tom Hauck/Allsport/Getty Images Sport/Getty Images, 13; Eliot J. Schechter/Allsport/Getty Images Sport/Getty Images, 15; Jeff Vinnick/Getty Images Sport/Getty Images, 16; Otto Greule Jr./Getty Images Sport/Getty Images, 19; Tim Clayton/Corbis Sport/Getty Images, 20; Emilee Chinn/Getty Images Sport/Getty Images, 22; Michael Reaves/Getty Images Sport/Getty Images, 25, 29; Alex Slitz/Getty Images Sport/Getty Images, 26

Press Box Books, an imprint of Press Room Editions.

ISBN
979-8-89469-011-7 (library bound)
979-8-89469-024-7 (paperback)
979-8-89469-049-0 (epub)
979-8-89469-037-7 (hosted ebook)

Library of Congress Control Number: 2025930337

Distributed by North Star Editions, Inc.
2297 Waters Drive
Mendota Heights, MN 55120
www.northstareditions.com

Printed in the United States of America
082025

ABOUT THE AUTHOR

Luke Hanlon is a sportswriter and editor based in Minneapolis. He's written dozens of nonfiction sports books for kids and spends a lot of his free time watching his favorite Minnesota sports teams.

TABLE of CONTENTS

CHAPTER 1
STAYING ALIVE   **5**

CHAPTER 2
ORLANDO ORIGINS   **11**

CHAPTER 3
RISING SUN   **17**

CHAPTER 4
CONSISTENT CONTENDERS   **23**

SUPERSTAR PROFILE
ALYSSA THOMAS   **28**

QUICK STATS	**30**
GLOSSARY	**31**
TO LEARN MORE	**32**
INDEX	**32**

CHAPTER 1

STAYING ALIVE

Alyssa Thomas drove hard into the paint. Three Las Vegas Aces defenders swarmed her. Thomas had no space to shoot. So, she whipped a pass out to Natisha Hiedeman. The Connecticut Sun guard buried the open three-pointer.

The Sun were hosting the Aces in Game 3 of the 2022 Women's National

Natisha Hiedeman averaged 7.5 points per game during the 2022 Finals

Basketball Association (WNBA) Finals. Las Vegas had won the first two games of the series. A loss would end Connecticut's season. However, the Aces jumped out to an early 12–4 lead. Hiedeman's three-pointer cut the Sun's deficit to five points.

Thomas continued to set up her teammates in the first quarter. After Hiedeman's bucket, Thomas assisted the next three Sun baskets. Late in the first quarter, Thomas buried a layup to put the Sun up by 13.

The Sun increased their lead to 23 points in the second quarter. But Las Vegas refused to give up. By the start of the fourth quarter, the Aces trailed

Alyssa Thomas racked up 31 assists in the 2022 Finals.

by only eight. Thomas wouldn't let them get any closer.

Early in the fourth quarter, Thomas tipped a Las Vegas pass. She stole the ball and burst down the court. An Aces

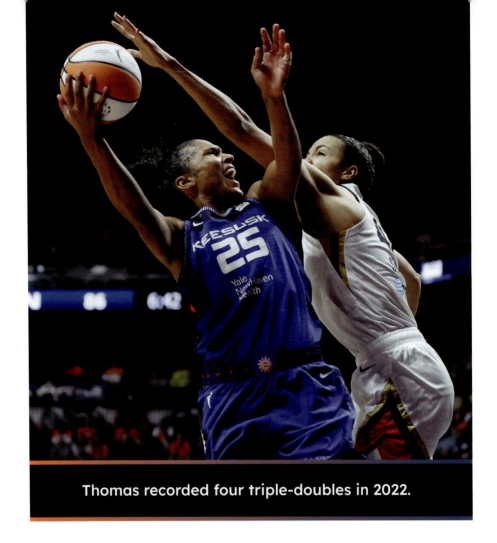

Thomas recorded four triple-doubles in 2022.

defender fouled Thomas while she tried to make a layup. The ball fell through the hoop anyway.

On the Sun's next possession, Thomas set up the offense. She saw DeWanna Bonner cutting toward the basket.

Thomas lobbed a pass to her. Bonner's layup made history for Thomas. That bucket gave Thomas 10 assists in the game. And she had already racked up 14 points and 12 rebounds. Those stats made her the first player to record a triple-double in WNBA Finals history.

The Sun easily closed out the game. They won 105–76 to force a Game 4. With Thomas leading the way, the Sun always had a chance to win.

TRIPLE-DOUBLE MACHINE

The first WNBA Finals took place in 1997. It took 25 years for a player to record a triple-double in the series. But it only took three days for someone to register another one. In Game 4, Thomas racked up 11 points, 11 assists, and 10 rebounds. However, the Aces won the game to clinch the title.

CHAPTER 2

ORLANDO ORIGINS

The history of the Connecticut Sun began in Orlando, Florida. Before the 1999 season, the WNBA added two new teams. The Orlando Miracle were one of them.

Expansion teams often struggle at first. But the WNBA wanted its new teams to be competitive. So, the league assigned Nykesha Sales

Nykesha Sales played in the All-Star Game each season during the first five years of her career.

to the Miracle. Sales had starred at the University of Connecticut (UConn). She finished as the school's all-time leading scorer. Her scoring skills carried over to the WNBA.

Sales earned a spot in the All-Star Game as a rookie. And she helped the Miracle come close to a playoff spot in their first season. Sales had plenty of help. Guard Shannon Johnson ran Orlando's offense. Taj McWilliams-Franklin provided tough defense. These two players joined Sales in the 1999 All-Star Game.

Orlando's star trio helped the team improve in 2000. The Miracle made the playoffs for the first time. They faced the Cleveland Rockers in the first round.

Shannon Johnson averaged 14 points per game in 1999.

In Game 1, McWilliams-Franklin recorded 16 points and 10 rebounds. She lifted Orlando to a 62–55 win. After that, the series moved to Cleveland. The Rockers won the next two games to eliminate the Miracle.

Orlando missed the playoffs for the next two seasons. During those years, the team lost money. So, the owners sold the Miracle. The Mohegan Tribe bought the team. The tribe became the first Indigenous group to own a professional sports team. In 2003, the tribe moved the team to Uncasville, Connecticut. Later that year, the Connecticut Sun played their first WNBA season.

CONNECTICUT TIES

UConn's women's basketball team became a powerhouse in the 1990s. UConn home games regularly sold out. The WNBA took notice. For years, the league pushed to bring a team to Connecticut. When the Miracle went up for sale, moving to Connecticut made the most sense. Fans flocked to Sun games to watch former UConn star Nykesha Sales.

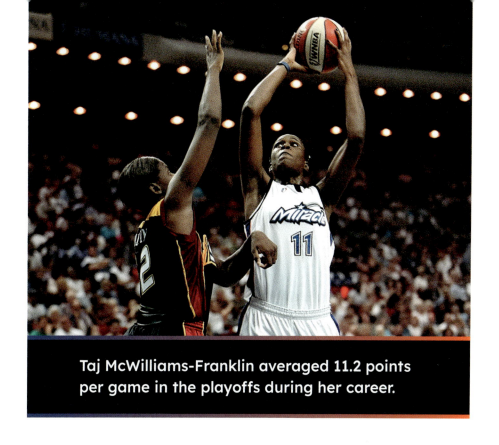

Taj McWilliams-Franklin averaged 11.2 points per game in the playoffs during her career.

The Sun made it back to the playoffs in 2003. There, McWilliams-Franklin took over. She hit a game-winning shot in Game 1 against the Charlotte Sting. Then she led the Sun with 16 points in Game 2. Her scoring helped secure the team's first playoff series victory. The Sun fell in the next round. But their future looked bright.

CHAPTER 3

RISING SUN

Before the 2004 season, the Sun traded away Shannon Johnson. In return, they received multiple draft picks. With one of them, Connecticut selected guard Lindsay Whalen. The move paid off quickly.

Whalen connected with fellow guard Katie Douglas. The duo helped the Sun reach the WNBA Finals in 2004.

Lindsay Whalen averaged 4.8 assists per game as a rookie.

Sun fans then watched their team win Game 1 against the Seattle Storm. However, Seattle won the new two games to claim the title.

The Sun gained valuable experience from the deep playoff run. It helped them sweep the first two rounds of the 2005 playoffs. Once again, Connecticut reached the Finals.

The Sacramento Monarchs beat the Sun in Game 1. In Game 2, Brooke Wyckoff stepped up for Connecticut. The forward hit a game-tying three-pointer in the final seconds. That shot sent the game to overtime. The Sun didn't allow a single point in the extra period. That helped seal the win. However, the Sun lost

Katie Douglas played in the All-Star Game twice with the Sun.

the next two games. For the second year in a row, they came up just short of a title.

After that, Connecticut's roster began to change. The team traded away Taj McWilliams-Franklin after the 2006 season. A year later, the Sun traded Douglas, too. Then Connecticut made a huge move in 2010. The team traded

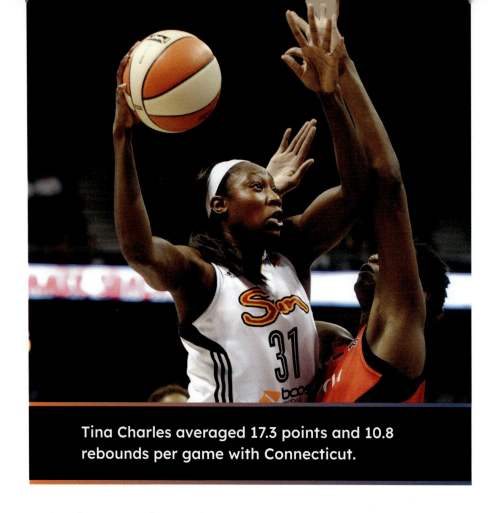

Tina Charles averaged 17.3 points and 10.8 rebounds per game with Connecticut.

Whalen to the Minnesota Lynx. In return, Connecticut received Renee Montgomery and the top pick in the 2010 draft.

The timing of the trade worked well for the Sun. They used the top draft pick on UConn star Tina Charles. Many Sun fans already adored their new star. Charles gave them plenty to cheer about. She averaged a double-double in her first four seasons in the league. In 2012, she earned the league's Most Valuable Player (MVP) Award.

Charles helped the Sun reach the semifinals in 2012. But Connecticut missed the playoffs in 2013. After that season, Charles demanded a trade. Soon, Sun fans would fall in love with a new star.

LOST POTENTIAL

The Sun drafted Chiney Ogwumike with the top pick in 2014. She won Rookie of the Year honors that year. When she was on the court, Ogwumike proved to be one of the league's best players. But injuries slowed her down. Ogwumike spent only three seasons with Connecticut.

CHAPTER 4

CONSISTENT CONTENDERS

The Sun received forward Alyssa Thomas as part of the Tina Charles trade. Thomas showed promise early in her career. Then she broke out in 2017. Thomas made her first All-Star Game that season.

Thomas thrived while playing alongside Jonquel Jones. The 6-foot-6 (198-cm) center controlled

In 2017, Alyssa Thomas made the WNBA All-Defensive Second Team.

games in the paint. She could also drain three-pointers. Thomas and Jones led the Sun back to the playoffs in 2017 and 2018. But both times, they fell in the second round.

By 2019, Thomas and Jones were two of the league's best defenders. They proved it in the playoffs. Thomas racked up steals in the semifinals against the Los Angeles Sparks. Meanwhile, Jones blocked seven shots in the series. The Sun swept the Sparks to advance to the Finals.

Connecticut faced off against the Washington Mystics in the Finals. The series went to a decisive Game 5. Thomas and Jones combined for 46 points in the

Jonquel Jones averaged 16.1 points per game in 26 playoff games with Connecticut.

game. However, the Mystics came out on top.

The Sun believed they had a team that could win a championship. So, they decided to go all in. Connecticut traded three first-round picks to the Phoenix Mercury. In return, the Sun got DeWanna Bonner.

In 2024, DeWanna Bonner (24) played in her third All-Star Game with Connecticut.

The veteran forward provided more size and scoring for the Sun. But it took a while before she played with all of Connecticut's other stars. Jones missed the 2020 season. Then Thomas played only three games in 2021.

Fully healthy in 2022, the Sun played in two tight playoff series. In the first round, they eliminated the Wings in Dallas. They then won a Game 5 on the road against the Chicago Sky. But the Las Vegas Aces ended the Sun's title hopes in the Finals.

Jones requested a trade after the 2022 season. Without her, the Sun still returned to the semifinals in 2023 and 2024. However, Bonner and Thomas left Connecticut after the 2024 season. Sun fans hoped to see new stars try to lift their team to a title.

FULL CIRCLE

The Sun started a rebuild after the 2024 season. Connecticut traded away three starters from the 2024 roster. The other two starters left in free agency. But one star returned to Connecticut. The Sun signed Tina Charles as a free agent. She had played for five other teams since the Sun traded her in 2014.

SUPERSTAR PROFILE

ALYSSA THOMAS

Alyssa Thomas began her career as a role player for the Sun. She eventually developed into one of the league's best players. And she helped improve the Sun along the way.

Thomas had few weaknesses. On offense, she loved showing off her passing skills. Thomas often looked to set up teammates. She had no problem scoring, either. Thomas drained mid-range jumpers with ease.

Thomas always fought for rebounds, too. That trait, along with her offensive skills, helped her stack up triple-doubles. In 2024, Thomas recorded the 15th of her career. No one else in WNBA history had more than four.

Thomas earned the nickname "The Engine." That's because she never stopped on defense. In 2024, Thomas made the All-Defensive Team for the sixth time.

Thomas made the All-WNBA First Team in 2023 and 2024.

QUICK STATS

CONNECTICUT SUN

Team History: Orlando Miracle (1999–2002), Connecticut Sun (2003–)

Championships: 0

Key coaches:
- Mike Thibault (2003–12): 206–134, 20–18 playoffs
- Curt Miller (2016–22): 140–86, 16–17 playoffs
- Stephanie White (2023–24): 55–25, 7–7 playoffs

Most career points: Nykesha Sales (3,955)

Most career assists: Alyssa Thomas (1,462)

Most career rebounds: Alyssa Thomas (2,395)

Most career blocks: Jonquel Jones (270)

Most career steals: Alyssa Thomas (494)

Stats are accurate through the 2024 season.

GLOSSARY

draft
An event that allows teams to choose new players coming into the league.

expansion teams
New teams that are added to an existing league.

free agent
A player who can sign with any team.

mid-range
The area of the court inside the three-point line and outside of the paint.

paint
The area between the basket and the free-throw line.

rookie
A first-year player.

sweep
To win all the games in a series.

triple-double
When a player reaches 10 or more of three different statistics in one game.

veteran
A player who has spent several years in a league.

TO LEARN MORE

Hanlon, Luke. *Everything Basketball*. Abdo Publishing, 2024.

O'Neal, Ciara. *The WNBA Finals*. Apex Editions, 2023.

Whiting, Jim. *The Story of the Connecticut Sun*. Creative Education, 2024.

MORE INFORMATION

To learn more about the Connecticut Sun, go to **pressboxbooks.com/AllAccess**. These links are routinely monitored and updated to provide the most current information available.

INDEX